THE POCKET HAVAMAL

ᚺᚨᚠᚠᚨᛗᚪᛚ

Benjamin Thorpe
Version

Copyright 2013
Huginn and Muninn Publishing
This book is part of the *Pocket Havamal©* series
All Rights Reserved

For information on Asatru and Germanic Heathenry please visit our website:

huginnandmuninn.net

Hail the Aesir!
Hail the Vanir!
Hail the Folk!

HAVAMAL
ᚺᚨᚠᚠᚨᛗᚨᛚ

1. All door-ways, before going forward, should be looked to; for difficult it is to know where foes may sit within a dwelling.

2. Givers, hail! A guest is come in: where shall he sit? In much haste is he, who on the ways has to try his luck.

3. Fire is needful to him who is come in, and whose knees are frozen; food and raiment a man requires, wheo'er the fell has travelled.

4. Water to him is needful who for refection comes, a towel and hospitable invitation, a good reception; if he can get it, discourse and answer.

5. Wit is needful to him who travels far: at home all is easy. A laughing-stock is he who nothing knows, and with the instructed sits.

6. Of his understanding no one should be proud, but rather in conduct cautious. When the prudent and taciturn come to a dwelling, harm seldom befalls the cautious; for a firmer friend no man ever gets than great discernment.

7. A wary guest, who to refection comes, keeps a cautious silence, with his ears listens, and with his eyes observes: so explores every prudent man.

8. He is happy, who for himself obtains fame and kind words: less sure is that which a man must have in another's breast.

9. He is happy, who in himself possesses fame and wit while living; for bad counsels have oft been received from another's heart.

10. A better burden no man bears on the road than much good sense; that is thought better than riches in a strange place; such is the recourse of the indigent.

11. A worse provision on the way he cannot carry than too much beer-bibbing; so good is not, as it is said, beer for the sons of men.

12. A worse provision no man can take from table than too much beer-bibbing: for the more he drinks the less control he has of his own mind.

13. Oblivion's heron 'tis called that over drink hovers; he steals the minds of men. With this bird's pinions I was fettered in Gunnlods dwelling.

14. Drunk I was, I was over-drunk, at that cunning Fialar's. It's the best drunkenness, when everyone after it regains his reason.

15. Taciturn and prudent, and in war daring, should a king's children be; joyous and generous everyone should be until his hour of death.

16. A cowardly man thinks he will ever live, if warfare he avoids; but old age will give him no peace, though spears may spare him.

17. A fool gapes when to a house he comes, to himself mutters or is silent; but all at once, if he gets drink, then is the man's mind displayed.

18. He alone knows who wanders wide, and has much experienced, by what disposition each man is ruled, who common sense possesses.

19. Let a man hold the cup, yet of the mead drink moderately, speak sensibly or be silent. As of a fault no man will admonish thee, if thou goest to bed early.

20. A greedy man, if he be not moderate, eats to his mortal sorrow. Oftentimes his belly draws laughter on a silly man, who among the prudent comes.

21. Cattle know when to go home, and then from grazing cease; but a foolish man never knows the measure of his own stomach.

22. A miserable man, and ill-conditioned, sneers at everything: one thing he knows not, which he ought to know, that he is not free from faults.

23. A foolish man is all night awake, pondering over everything; he then grows tired; and when morning comes, all is lament as before.

24. A foolish man thinks all who on him smile to be his friends; he feels it not, although they speak ill of him, when he sits among the clever.

25. A foolish man thinks all who speak him fair to be his friends; but he will find, if into court he comes, that he has few advocates.

26. A foolish man thinks he knows everything if placed in unexpected difficulty; but he knows not what to answer, if to the test he is put.

27. A foolish man, who among people comes, had best be silent; for no one knows that he knows nothing, unless he talks too much. He who previously knew nothing will still know nothing, talk he ever so much.

28. He thinks himself wise, who can ask questions and converse also; conceal his ignorance no one can, because it circulates among men.

29. He utters too many futile words who is never silent; a garrulous tongue, if it be not checked, sings often to its own harm.

30. For a gazing-stock no man shall have another, although he come a stranger to his house. Many a one thinks himself wise, if he is not questioned, and can sit in a dry habit.

31. Clever thinks himself the guest who jeers a guest, if he takes to flight. Knows it not certainly he who prates at meat, whether he babbles among foes.

32. Many men are mutually well-disposed, yet at table will torment each other. That strife will ever be; guest will guest irritate.

33. Early meals a man should often take, unless to a friend's house he goes; else he will sit and mope, will seem half-famished, and can of few things inquire.

34. Long is and indirect the way to a bad friend's, though by the road he dwell; but to a good friend's the paths lie direct, though he lives far away.

35. A guest should depart, not always stay in one place. The guest becomes unwelcome, if he too long stays in another's house.

36. One's own house is best, small though it be; at home is everyone his own master. Though he but two goats possess, and a straw-thatched cot, even that is better than begging.

37. One's own house is best, small though it be, at home is everyone his own master. Bleeding at heart is he, who has to ask for food at every meal-tide.

38. Leaving in the field his arms, let no man go a foot's length forward; for it is hard to know when on the way a man may need his weapon.

39. I have never found a man so wealthy, or so hospitable that he refused a gift; or of his property so abundant that he scorned a repayment.

40. Of the property which he has gained no man should suffer need; for the hated oft is spared what for the dear was destined. Much goes worse than is expected.

41. With arms and vestments friends should each other gladden, those which are in themselves most sightly. Givers and requiters are longest friends, if all goes well.

42. To his friend a man should be a friend, and gifts with gifts requite. Laughter with laughter men should receive, but repay treachery with lies.

43. To his friend a man should be a friend; to him and to his friend; but of his foe no man shall the friend's friend be.

44. Know, if thou hast a friend whom thou fully trustest, and from whom thou woulds't good derive, thou shouldst blend thy mind with his, and gifts exchange, and often go to see him.

45. If thou hast another, whom thou little trustest, yet wouldst good from him derive, thou shouldst speak him fair, but think craftily, and repay treachery with lies.

46. But of him yet further, whom thou little trustest, and thou suspectest his intention; before him thou shouldst laugh, and contrary to thy thoughts speak: requital should the gift resemble.

47. I was once young, I was journeying alone, and lost my way; rich I thought myself, when I met another. Man is the joy of man.

48. Generous and brave men live best, they seldom cherish sorrow; but a base-minded man dreads everything; the niggardly is uneasy even at gifts.

49. My garments in a field I gave away to two wooden men: heroes they seemed to be, when they got cloaks: exposed to insult is a naked man.

50. A tree withers that on a hill-top stands; protects it neither bark nor leaves: such is the man whom no one favours: why should he live long?

51. Hotter than fire love for five days burns between false friends; but is quenched when the sixth day comes, and-friendship is all impaired.

52. Something great is not always to be given, praise is often for a trifle bought. With half a loaf and a tilted vessel I got myself a comrade.

53. Little are the sand-grains, little the wits, little the minds of some men; for all men are not wise alike: men are everywhere by halves.

54. Moderately wise should each one be, but never over-wise: of those men the lives are fairest, who know much well.

55. Moderately wise should each one be, but never over-wise; for a wise man's heart is seldom glad, if he is all-wise who owns it.

56. Moderately wise should each one be, but never over-wise. His destiny let know no man beforehand; his mind will be freest from' care.

57. Brand burns from brand until it is burnt out; fire is from fire quickened. Man to' man becomes known by speech, but a fool by his bashful silence.

58. He should early rise, who another's property or life desires to have. Seldom a sluggish wolf gets prey, or a sleeping man victory.

59. Early should rise he who has few workers, and go his work to see to; greatly is he retarded who sleeps the morn away. Wealth half depends on energy.

60. Of dry planks and roof-shingles a man knows the measure; of the fire-wood that may suffice, both measure and time.

61. Washed and well-fed let a man ride to the Thing, although his garments be not too good; of his shoes and breeches let no one be ashamed, nor of his horse, although he have not a good one.

62. Inquire and impart should every man of sense, who will be accounted sage. Let one only know, a second may not; if three, all the world knows.

63. Gasps and gapes, when to the sea he comes, the eagle over old ocean; so is a man, who among many comes, and has few advocates.

64. His power should every wise man use with discretion; for he will find, when among the bold he comes, that no one alone is bravest.

65. Prudent and reserved every man should be, and wary in trusting friends. Of the words that a man says to another he often pays the penalty.

66. Much too early I came to many places, but too late to others: the beer was drunk, or not yet brewed: the disliked seldom chooses the right moment.

67. Here and there I should have been invited, if I a meal had needed; or two hams had hung, at that true friend's, where of one I had eaten.

68. Fire is best among the sons of men, and the sight of the sun, if his health a man can have, with a life free from vice.

69. No man lacks everything, although his health be bad: one in his sons is happy, one in his kin, one in abundant wealth, one in his good works.

70. It is better to live, even to live miserably; a living man can always get a cow. I saw fire consume the rich man's property, and death stood without his door.

71. The halt can ride on horseback, the one-handed drive cattle; the deaf fight and be useful: to be blind is better than to be burnt no one gets good from a corpse.

72. A son is better, even if born late, after his father's departure. Gravestones seldom stand by the way-side unless raised by a kinsman to a kinsman.

73. Two are adversaries: the tongue is the bane of the head: under every cloak I expect a sword.

74. At night is joyful he who is sure of travelling entertainment. A ship's yards are short. Variable is an autumn night. Many are the weather's changes in five days, but more in a month.

75. He only knows not who knows nothing, that many a one apes another. One man is rich, another poor: let him not be thought blameworthy.

76. Cattle die, kindred die, we ourselves also die; but the fair fame never dies of him who has earned it.

77. Cattle die, kindred die, we ourselves also die; but I know one thing that never dies,—judgment on each one dead.

78. Full storehouses I saw at Dives' sons': now bear they the beggar's staff. Such are riches; as is the twinkling of an eye: of friends they are most fickle.

79. A foolish man, if he acquires wealth or woman's love, pride grows within him, but wisdom never: he goes on more and more arrogant.

80. Then 'tis made manifest, if of runes thou questionest him, those to the high ones known, which the great powers invented, and the great talker painted, that he had best hold silence.

81. At eve the day is to be praised, a woman after she is burnt, a sword after it is proved, a maid after she is married, ice after it has passed away, beer after it is drunk.

82. In the wind one should hew wood, in a breeze row out to sea, in the dark talk with a lass: many are the eyes of day. In a ship voyages are to be made, but a shield is for protection, a sword for striking, but a damsel for a kiss.

83. By the fire one should drink beer, on the ice slide; buy a horse that is lean, a sword that is rusty; feed a horse at home, but a dog at the farm.

84. In a maiden's words no one should place faith, nor in what a woman says; for on a turning wheel have their hearts been formed, and guile in their breasts been laid;

85. In a creaking bow, a burning flame, a yawning wolf, a chattering crow, a grunting swine, a rootless tree, a waxing wave, a boiling kettle,

86. A flying dart, a falling billow, a one night's ice, a coiled serpent, a woman's bed-talk, or a broken sword, a bear's play, or a royal child,

87. A sick calf, a self-willed thrall, a flattering prophetess, a corpse newly slain, a serene sky, a laughing lord, a barking dog, and a harlot's grief;

88. An early sown field let no one trust, nor prematurely in a son: weather rules the field, and wit the son, each of which is doubtful;

89. A brother's murderer, though on the high road met, a half-burnt house, an over-swift horse, (a horse is useless, if a leg be broken), no man is so confiding as to trust any of these.

90. Such is the love of women, who falsehood meditate, as if one drove not rough-shod, on slippery ice, a spirited two-years old and unbroken horse; or as in a raging storm a helmless ship is beaten; or as if the halt were set to catch a reindeer in the thawing fell.

91. Openly I now speak, because I both sexes know: unstable are men's minds towards women; 'tis then we speak most fair when we most falsely think: that deceives even the cautious.

92. Fair shall speak, and money offer, who would obtain a woman's love. Praise the form of a fair damsel; he gets who courts her.

93. At love should no one ever wonder in another: a beauteous countenance oft captivates the wise, which captivates not the foolish.

94. Let no one wonder at another's folly, it is the lot of many. All-powerful desire makes of the sons of men fools even of the wise.

95. The mind only knows what lies near the heart, that alone is conscious of our affections. No disease is worse to a sensible man than not to be content with himself.

96. That I experienced, when in the reeds I sat, awaiting my delight. Body and soul to me was that discreet maiden: nevertheless I possess her not.

97. Billing's lass on her couch I found, sun-bright, sleeping. A prince's joy to me seemed naught, if not with that form to live.

98. "Yet nearer eve must thou, Odin, come, if thou wilt talk the maiden over; all will be disastrous, unless we alone are privy to such misdeed."

99. I returned, thinking to love, at her wise desire. I thought I should obtain her whole heart and love.

100. When next I came the bold warriors were all awake, with lights burning, and bearing torches: thus was the way to pleasure closed.

101. But at the approach of morn, when again I came, the household all was sleeping; the good damsel's dog alone I found tied to the bed.

102. Many a fair maiden, when rightly known, towards men is fickle: that I experienced, when that discreet maiden I strove to seduce: insults of every sort that wily girl heaped upon me; though nothing of that damsel did I gain.

103. At home let a man be cheerful, and towards a guest generous; of wise conduct he should be, of good memory and ready speech; if much knowledge he desires, he must often talk on good.

104. Fimbulfambi he is called who' little has to say: such is the nature of the simple.

105. The old Jotun I sought; now I am come back: little got I there by silence; in many words I spoke to my advantage in Suttung's halls.

106. Gunnlod gave me, on her golden seat, a draught of the precious mead; a bad recompense I afterwards made her, for her whole soul, her fervent love.

107. Rati's mouth I caused to make a space, and to gnaw the rock; over and under me were the Jotun's ways: thus I my head did peril.

108. Of a well-assumed form I made good use: few things fail the wise; for Odhrærir is now come up to men's earthly dwellings.

109. 'Tis to me doubtful that I could have come from the Jotun's courts, had not Gunnlod aided me, that good damsel, over whom I laid my arm.

110. On the day following came the Hrimthursar, to learn something of the High One, in the High One's hall: after Bolverk they inquired, whether he with the gods were come, or Suttung had destroyed him?

111. Odin, I believe, a ring-oath gave. Who in his faith will trust? Suttung defrauded, of his drink bereft, and Gunnlod made to weep!

112. Time 'tis to speak from the wise one's chair. By the well of Urd I silent sat, I saw and meditated, I listened to men's words.

113. Of runes I heard discourse, and of things divine, nor of graving them were they silent, nor of sage counsels, at the High One's hall. In the High One's hall. I thus heard say:

114. I counsel thee, Loddfafnir, to take advice: thou wilt profit if thou takest it. Rise not at night, unless to explore, or art compelled to go out.

115. I counsel thee, Loddfafnir, to take advice, thou wilt profit if thou takest it. In an enchantress's embrace thou mayest not sleep, so that in her arms she clasp thee.

116. She will be the cause that thou carest not for Thing or prince's words; food thou wilt shun and human joys; sorrowful wilt thou go to sleep.

117. I counsel thee, Loddfafnir, to take advice, thou wilt profit if thou takest it. Another's wife entice thou never to secret converse.

118. I counsel thee, Loddfafnir, to take advice, thou wilt profit if thou takest it. By fell or firth if thou have to travel, provide thee well with food.

119. I counsel thee, Loddfafnir, to take advice, thou wilt profit if thou takest it. A bad man let thou never know thy misfortunes; for from a bad man thou never wilt obtain a return for thy good will.

120. I saw mortally wound a man a wicked woman's words; a false tongue caused his death, and most unrighteously.

121. I counsel thee, Loddfafnir, to take advice, thou wilt profit if thou takest it. If thou knowest thou hast a friend, whom thou well canst trust, go oft to visit him; for with brushwood over-grown, and with high grass, is the way that no one treads.

122. I counsel thee, Loddfafnir, to take advice, thou wilt profit if thou takest it. A good man attract to thee in pleasant converse; and salutary speech learn while thou livest.

123. I counsel thee, Loddfafnir, to take advice, thou wilt profit if thou takest it. With thy friend be thou never first to quarrel. Care gnaws the heart, if thou to no one canst thy whole mind disclose.

124. I counsel thee, Loddfafnir, to take advice, thou wilt profit if thou takest it. Words thou never shouldst exchange with a witless fool;

125. For from an ill-conditioned man thou wilt never get a return for good; but a good man will bring thee favour by his praise.

126. There is a mingling of affection, where one can tell another all his mind. Everything is better than being with the deceitful. He is not another's friend who ever says as he says.

127. I counsel thee, Loddfafnir, to take advice, thou wilt profit if thou takest it. Even in three words quarrel not with a worse man: often the better yields, when the worse strikes.

128. I counsel thee, Loddfafnir, to take advice, thou wilt profit if thou takest it. Be not a shoemaker, nor a shaftmaker, unless for thyself it be; for a shoe if ill made, or a shaft if crooked, will call down evil on thee.

129. I counsel thee, Loddfafnir, to take advice, thou wilt profit if thou takest it. Wherever of injury thou knowest, regard that injury as thy own; and give to thy foes no peace.

130. I counsel thee, Loddfafnir, to take advice, thou wilt profit if thou takest it. Rejoiced at evil be thou never; but let good give thee pleasure.

131. I counsel thee, Loddfafnir, to take advice, thou wilt profit if thou takest it. In a battle look not up, (like swine the sons of men then become) that men may not fascinate thee.

132. If thou wilt induce a good woman to pleasant converse, thou must promise fair, and hold to it: no one turns from good if it can be got.

133. I enjoin thee to be wary, but not over wary; at drinking be thou most wary, and with another's wife; and thirdly, that thieves delude thee not.

134. With insult or derision treat thou never a guest or wayfarer. They often little know, who sit within, of what race they are who come.

135. Vices and virtues the sons of mortals bear in their breasts mingled; no one is so good that no failing attends him, nor so bad as to be good for nothing.

136. At a elder speaker laugh thou never; often is good that which the aged utter, oft from a shriveled hide discreet words issue; from those whose skin is sagging and decked with scars, and who go tottering among the vile.

137. I counsel thee, Loddfafnir, to take advice, thou wilt profit if thou takest it. Rail not at a guest, nor from thy gate thrust him; treat well the indigent; they will speak well of thee.

138. Strong is the bar that must be raised to admit all. Do thou give a penny, or they will call down on thee every ill in thy limbs.

139. I counsel thee, Loddfafnir, to take advice, thou wilt profit if thou takest it. Wherever thou beer drinkest, invoke to thee the power of earth; for earth is good against drink, fire for distempers, the oak for constipation, a corn-ear for sorcery, a hall for domestic strife. In bitter hates invoke the moon; the biter for bite-injuries is good; but runes against calamity; fluid let earth absorb.

ODIN'S RUNE POEM
ᛟᛞᛁᚺᛋ ᚱᚨᛏᛗ ᚲᛟᛗᚺ

140. I know that I hung, on a wind-swept tree, nine whole nights, with a spear wounded, and to Odin offered, myself to myself; on that tree, of which no one knows from what root it springs.

141. Bread no one gave me, nor a horn of drink, downward I peered, to runes applied myself, wailing learnt them, then fell down thence.

142. Potent songs nine from the famed son I learned of Bolthorn, Bestla's sire, and a draught obtained of the precious mead, drawn from Odhrærir.

143. Then I began to bear fruit, and to know many things, to grow and well thrive: word by word I sought out words, fact by fact I sought out facts.

144. Runes thou wilt find, and explained characters, very large characters, very potent characters, which the great speaker depicted, and the high powers formed, and the powers' prince graved:

145. Odin among the Æsir, but among the Alfar, Dain, and Dvalin for the dwarfs, Asvid for the Jotuns: some I myself carved.

146. Knowest thou how to carve them? knowest thou how to expound them? knowest thou how to depict them? knowest thou how to prove them? knowest thou how to invoke? knowest thou how to sacrifice? knowest thou how to send? knowest thou how to consume?

147. 'Tis better not to pray than too much sacrifice; a gift ever looks to a return. 'Tis better not to send than too much consume. So Thund carved before the origin of men, where he ascended, to whence he afterwards came.

148. Those songs I know which the king's wife knows not nor son of man. Help the first is called, for that will help thee against strifes and cares.

149. For the second I know, what the sons of men require, who will as leeches live.

150. For the third I know, if I have great need to restrain my foes, the weapons' edge I deaden: of my adversaries nor arms nor wiles harm aught.

151. For the fourth I know, if men place bonds on my limbs, I so sing that I can walk; the fetter falls from my feet, and the manacle from my hands.

152. For the fifth I know, if I see a shot from a hostile hand, a shaft flying amid the host, so swift it cannot fly that I cannot halt it, if only I get sight of it.

153. For the sixth I know, if one wounds me with a green tree's roots; also if a man declares hatred to me, harm shall consume them sooner than me.

154. For the seventh I know, if a lofty house I see blaze o'er its inmates, so furiously it shall not burn that I cannot save it. That song I can sing.

155. For the eighth I know, what to all is useful to learn: where hatred grows among the sons of men—that I can quickly mediate.

156. For the ninth I know, if I stand in need my bark on the water to save, I can the wind on the waves allay, and the sea lull.

157. For the tenth I know, if I see troll-wives sporting in air, I can so operate that they will forsake their own forms, and their own minds.

158. For the eleventh I know, if I have to lead my ancient friends to battle, under their shields I sing, and with power they go safe to the fight, safe from the fight; safe on every side they go.

159. For the twelfth I know, if on a tree I see a corpse swinging from a halter, I can so carve and in runes depict, that the man shall walk, and with me converse.

160. For the thirteenth I know, if on a young man I sprinkle water, he shall not fall, though he into battle come: that man shall not sink before swords.

161. For the fourteenth I know, if in the society of men I have to name the gods, Æsir and Alfar, I know the distinctions of all. This few unskilled can do.

162. For the fifteenth I know what the dwarf Thiodreyrir sang before Delling's doors. Strength he sang to the Æsir, and to the Alfar prosperity, wisdom to Hroptatyr.

163. For the sixteenth I know, if a modest maiden's favour and affection I desire to possess, the soul I change of the white-armed damsel, and wholly turn her mind.

164. For the seventeenth I know, that that young maiden will reluctantly avoid me. These songs, Loddfafnir! thou wilt long have lacked; yet it may be good if thou understandest them, profitable if thou learnest them.

165. For the eighteenth I know that which I never teach to maid or wife of man, (all is better what one only knows. This is the closing of the songs) save her alone who clasps me in her arms, or is my sister.

166. Now are sung the High-one's songs, in the High-one's hall, to the sons of men all-useful, but useless to the Jotuns' sons. Hail to him who has sung them! Hail to him who knows them! May he profit who has learnt them! Hail to those who have listened to them!

TOTMS

NOTES

TOTMS

NOTES

TOTEMS

Printed in Great Britain
by Amazon

51559732R00030